JoAnna Carey's

Rat Race Relaxer:
Your Potential &
The Maze of Life

© 2003 JoAnna Carey
Published by Carey'D Away Enterprises, LLC
2455 Woodlake Road SW, Suite 4
Wyoming, MI 49509
Phone (616) 530-3787 Fax (616) 406-0944
www.RatRaceRelaxer.com

Editor: Morgan Jarema
Cover and Author Photos: Bernadine Carey-Tucker
Cover and Interior Layout: Susan Harring
Contributor: Karen Rosasco, APRN, BC. Family Nurse Practitioner at Wege
Institute for Mind, Body, and Spirit at St. Mary's Mercy Medical Center,
Grand Rapids, Michigan

Greatful acknowledgement is made to the following for permission to
reprint copyrighted material:
Bethards, Betty. *The Dream Book: Symbols For Self-Understanding*.
Pentaluma: NewCentury Publishers, 2001.

1. Business/Motivation
2. Self-Help
3. Stress Management

ISBN 0-9723715-0-8
LCCN 2002093857
Printed in the USA

Special Sales

Carey'D Away Enterprises, LLC
books are available at special discounts
for bulk purchase as sales promotions
or premiums.
Special editions including personalized
covers, excerpts of existing books and
corporate imprints can be created in
large quantities for special needs.

For more information write to:

V.P. of Sales & Marketing
Carey'D Away Enterprises, LLC
2455 Woodlake Road SW, Suite 4
Wyoming, MI 49509

(616) 530-3787
j.carey@att.net
www.RatRaceRelaxer.com

Dedication

For anyone who has become lost or disoriented while racing through this maze of life, I hope this becomes your roadmap. It is especially designed for those who never like to stop to ask for directions.

Acknowledgements

I found my voice for this book through the support and encouragement of my loving family, friends, mentors and teachers.

Steve, my best friend and husband, there is no end to your strength, support and encouragement. Thank you for loving me for who I am and for making me laugh until my face hurts. You are my sunshine.

For my beautiful mom, Gail, you generously dedicate all your energy to taking care of your family. Your career as a stay-at-home mom has directly contributed to my success. Thank you for teaching me to always be myself and choose what's right, not what's easy. You add the brightness of flowers and the joy of hummingbirds to my life.

To my brave dad, Daniel, you are my hero and my superman. I couldn't ask for a better partner. Thank you for teaching me that there are no limits to what a "girl" can accomplish. You bring the abundance of buffalo and spirit of the eagle to my life.

To Bernadine, my younger sister, you remind me to relax, follow my dreams and let happiness be my goal. Thank you for bringing out my best in the photo shoot for this book cover. Thanks, too, for having coffee with me when I really need a friend. You give me a reason to blaze trails.

To Todd, my brother-in-law, you challenge my theories and remind me that I sometimes think too much. With your help, I've learned to believe that most things will work out in their own way and in their own time. Thank you for introducing me to new ideas and for taking good care of my sister.

To my grandparents, Bernadine and William, who just celebrated fifty years of marriage, you have demonstrated the value of commitment and are always a big part of my daily life.

To my great-grandmothers, Gertrude and Virginia, I am glad you are still around to share stories and pass on the wisdom you've gained over the years.

To my grandmother, Florence, and great-grandfather, Vincent, you have passed on but are with me in spirit.

To my four generations of extended family and family through marriage — far too many to list, thank you for the wide variety of experiences you provide. Terri, thanks for being the first one to courageously work through each chapter to test the impact of implementing these keys.

To my mentors and friends who have entered my life at different stages but always at the exact moment I needed them to appear: Joanne Seminetta, Tom Hoiles, Paul Spaniola, Gregg Dimkoff, Jenny Shangraw, Cheryl Johnson, Shirley Hubers, Meredyth Parrish, Lynn Afendoulis and Annie Zimmerman.

And last but not least, thank you to Morgan Jarema, my editor, who stepped into my life just as this book was coming together and had already incorporated many of these same ideas into her own life. Her wisdom and experience added more merit than I can find words to express.

"True morality consists, not in following the beaten track, but in finding out the true path for ourselves and in fearlessly following it."
— Mohandas Gandhi

Navigating the Maze of Life

My own wake-up call came when I was just 25 years old. I was a financial advisor — a fully licensed stockbroker — in a Michigan branch of one of the largest investment firms on Wall Street. I had just closed a $2 million estate plan, resulting in over $13,000 in commissions.

At the time I thought it was my dream job. During training the year before, I learned that approximately 100 candidates were interviewed before even one was offered the opportunity to join the firm. I was proud; I believed that I had "made it." My hard work was paying off. This was my idea of the American dream – a prestigious corporate position, a shot at a window office and the potential to make enough money to retire early.

I was so committed to reaching the goals laid out in my performance review that I never stopped working. During my workdays I was on the phone, visiting business owners or meeting with potential clients. At home I was drafting marketing plans, searching for new prospecting ideas, reading journals to sharpen my skills or reviewing my day's work. I literally began to dream at night about closing deals and filling out new account forms.

My wake-up call began with the closing of the estate case. Next came advice from a seasoned broker that went something like this: " You have three choices at this point in your investment career: You can be at the office working, home having dinner with your husband or whomever else you choose, or sleeping. That's the kind of commitment you have to make if you want to be a success in this business." After the initial shock and anger subsided, I realized that working, eating and sleeping was exactly what my life had become.

I no longer laughed. I had no friends. I wasn't celebrating my accomplishments and was in desperate need of a vacation. This was not how I thought success should look or feel.

Being in the investment business requires absolute dedication; with no tolerance for the middle-of-the-road, my choice was to be in or out. Because I wasn't a seasoned advisor, vacation was discouraged. So I took a few weekends off to think about where I had been and where I wanted to go in my life.

I reviewed my performance for the year, which even with the estate case settlement was too low by industry standards, and realized that I couldn't fully buy into goals that I had no input in setting. After years of doing what others thought I should do, the faint at first, then intermittent ringing of my wake-up call became a ceaseless, wailing siren.

I know now that my path wouldn't have seemed so complicated if I had only known how to read my internal warning signs. I wasn't clear about what I wanted, so the desires of others began to consume my energy. I stopped taking time for myself, stopped exercising and gave up traveling.

In order to recognize my internal road signs, I had to embark on a journey of building an inventory of who I am, what I have to offer and what I want in return. I realized that in trying to assimilate into a corporate culture I was losing the very thing that gave me a competitive edge – the ability to be myself, an original. It didn't happen overnight, but I planned a vacation, resigned from my "dream job" and decided it was time to focus my attention on building my own business — on my own terms. On my journey, I discovered how to stop running, to relax into my unique path and to enjoy my individuality. I stopped letting the rat race run me and instead began using my skills to navigate through the maze of life. This book is a compilation of how I learned to love my life, imperfections and all.

Table of Contents

52 Keys To Unlock Your Potential In The Maze Of Life

Welcome

The Rat Race Relaxer is about choices. We make choices every day, from the moment we wake up until we fall into bed at night. Amid today's culture of information overload we are bombarded with so many choices we often wish we didn't have to decide. We have so many choices to make that we often let others decide for us so we don't have to feel responsible for making the wrong ones. But most importantly, when it comes to making the biggest decisions of our lives, I often hear people mutter, "I really don't have a choice." Our perceived powerlessness amid the myriad of available choices is what most often leads us to believe that the rat race can never be run on our own terms.

This is not a book about escaping the rat race; in my opinion, the rat race is inescapable. It is also not an attempt to help you build a more perfect life or a guide about how to leave all your stress behind. Instead, it is a journey to learn more about who you are. I hope that through these exercises you will begin to accept your mistakes, failures and imperfections as part of your unique path to success, and use this book as a toolbox to build skills that can help you deal more effectively within the chaos of an imperfect system.

I invite you to sit back, enjoy and use the keys that I present throughout this book to *relax into* the rat race and reflect upon how you indeed *can choose* the

things you want out of life. This book offers 52 keys —
one for every week of the year — that can unlock your
potential for making reasoned, proactive choices about
your life.

Don't be fooled by the simplicity of these keys. The
ease of incorporating them into your daily life is precisely
why they can help you find new meaning in your current
job, show you a path to a whole new journey or expose
the specific areas of your life that are causing unhealthy
levels of stress. I think the most effective way to
incorporate these concepts is by committing one week
to each key so they become more than just exercises;
the keys become habits. If you are averse to the thought
of change taking an entire year, then commit to a time
schedule that feels right for your situation. You'll see
results as you implement each key! This is your book
and your life, so set your own rules and work at your own
pace. Also, feel free to work on the keys in the order
that pertains the most to the areas of your life that
you would like to change first. If it does take you an
entire year, think of it this way: what's a year when it
means a happier rest of your life?

I don't pretend to have all the answers. I am here to
share stories of how my friends and I not only are
surviving the rat race, but how we're thriving and
succeeding. I love the thrill of the race, the uncertainty
of change and the challenge of reaching for new heights.
So how do I know this book works? Because I also slip

back into high stress habits and have used these keys to remind me that it is ok to slow down. By relaxing into where I am each day, I have learned how to plot my course through the maze of the future. And so can you!

You have the answers to your situation. So what are you waiting for? Use this book to reflect upon your potential in the maze of life. It's your time to discover and pursue your unique life mission. If you take only one thing away from this book, I want you to know that you *can* choose to change anything. Don't wait until tomorrow or next week; start today. Start right now.

Rat Race Relaxer

Chapter 1

Practice being open-minded

Just as every action has a reaction, every thought or idea has an effect on your future. Making snap judgments will often close off opportunities for growth. With an open mind, you will find new ways of seeing the world. By approaching people and events openly, we are able to experience life through the eyes of a child. Being open-minded does not necessarily mean agreeing with another's choice, but you can make it a habit to find the "gold" in other lifestyles and beliefs. This is especially useful when you are looking for a solution to a dilemma.

I try to surround myself with people from many different walks of life. I find that the more colorful the character, the more interesting the life story. By really listening to what others share about themselves, you will see a reflection of who you are now — and a glimmer of what you would like to become. Did you ever notice that when you're in a very negative mood, you tend to attract others who share only the negative things that surround them? A negative attitude is contagious, but so is a positive attitude. Practice being positive and you will see how others automatically want to tell you about the great things happening in their lives.

This Week's Key To Unlock Your Potential: Look for new ways to navigate the maze. For one whole week, try listening to others without defending your point of view or playing the devil's advocate. Document anything new that you learn.

Chapter 2

Be willing to share what you know

The easiest way to find others who will help you is by offering to share what you know. This can be as simple as sharing a recipe or as involved as volunteering to be a mentor. Especially in business settings, you often have to train your replacement in order to be promoted to the next level. Start sharing what you know now and watch new opportunities unfold.

If you find yourself hiding what you know, ask why. Are you afraid of being replaced, or of revealing knowledge that you believe guarantees your job security? Will sharing what you know really make you less valuable or less knowledgeable? Have you previously shared what you know only to have the situation backfire? Don't allow the malice of others to block your path, take what you can learn from unfriendly incidents and move on. When you believe that your skills and abilities are truly unique, you can spend less energy hoarding knowledge and more energy promoting what you know in an effort to reach personal goals.

When I worked as a financial advisor, I became saddened by how the constant search for new clients resulted in often ultra-competitive behavior among colleagues in the same office. One day I overheard a conversation between a mother-daughter financial advising team who worked across the hall. They were trying frantically to prepare a full-color chart for their next meeting and couldn't get the spreadsheet program to cooperate. I walked across the hall, explained that I overheard them discussing their problem and offered to help. Ten minutes later I had not only produced the chart they wanted, but showed both of them how to manipulate the program with just a couple keystrokes to produce overview charts for their other clients. Later, the same women offered to help me with ideas to market my own business and gave me one of their out-of-town accounts that didn't receive as many face-to-face meetings as they were usually able to provide. The account was worth more than $100,000.

This Week's Key To Unlock Your Potential:
Spend less energy hoarding knowledge and more energy promoting what you know in an effort to reach personal goals. Teach another how to do something that you love to do and ask that person to demonstrate something that you know he or she is good at.

Chapter 3

Reflect upon your life

We often hear people who have had a near-fatal accident, poor medical diagnosis or traumatic event share their stories of regret. In today's fast-paced society, we often don't take the time to ask ourselves where we have been, where we are going, whether the path we started down has somehow changed or if we have simply outgrown what we initially set out to do.

In college I had dreams of running my own business. I didn't know exactly what that business would be, but it was a daydream that I entertained every time I grew bored in class. When I entered the "real world," I gradually became bogged down in the negativity of those around me who were always ready with that catch-all phrase, "That's been done before, it will NEVER work!" I didn't realize how off course I had strayed until I found myself dreading my job every morning. It was that feeling of dread that finally forced me to acknowledge that I couldn't fully buy into goals that I had no input in setting. After years of doing what I thought I was "supposed" to do to be successful, I resigned from my corporate position. It took tremendous courage and energy to face the path I just completed, plan a new course of action and forge ahead in my own marketing consulting business. Had I not reflected upon the path I was walking, I wouldn't have seen the fork in the road. (See Chapter 40 for more on reflecting upon your life.)

This Week's Key To Unlock Your Potential: Take a breather from the rat race: think back to a time when you were 20 years old or younger, and write about what you thought your future life would look like. How does your current life compare to that earlier vision? Have you been pursuing the things you wanted to pursue? Now, write about something that you love about your life today that you never imagined in those earlier years.

Chapter 4

Experiment every day

Are you one of those people who take the same route to work every day? Do you always eat at the same restaurant? Do you choose the same parking space every time you visit your favorite haunts? If you always do things the same way, you will always get the same results. Be willing to try something new. If you don't like what you try, you've got a perfect reason to try something new the next day. If you do like what you try, it will give you the confidence to continue to search for other things that add joy to your life.

Steve is the kind of person who used to do the same things at the same time each day. He became bored and dissatisfied with the robotic feeling of simply carrying out a daily routine. So he began experimenting with the small things — such as carrying a pocket watch instead of wearing a wristwatch or shaving with a blade razor instead of his trusty electric shaver. Steve found that experimenting is not just a fun way to change his daily routine; it also makes it easier for him to look for and try new solutions to larger problems. Variety is the spice of life.

This Week's Key To Unlock Your Potential:
Try at least one new thing each day for the next seven days. Even if it is as simple as trying a different sandwich at lunchtime, push those comfortable boundaries of your habits. Don't give up if you don't like what you try, this week your challenge is to find something new that you do like.

Chapter 5

Be honest with yourself and others

Most of us were taught that it is wrong to lie to others. But were you ever told that it is wrong to lie to *yourself?* If you make excuses for all the things that make you unhappy but are too afraid to make the changes necessary to make reasoned, proactive choices, then you are living a lie! Be honest with yourself. If you're unhappy, start by admitting it to yourself, then take the first step TODAY. Begin the changes that will allow your life to bring you joy.

I see this dilemma often among parents with young children. Some are stay-at -home moms who would really like to work at least part-time. Others are working at careers that leave them unsatisfied, when they would really prefer to spend more time with their children. And although we don't often hear about this dilemma among fathers, there are a growing number of young men who are sharing equally in the day-to-day activities of child rearing and would also like more flexible work schedules. This is a classic example of taking the time to determine what is most important in your life and being honest with yourself.

This Week's Key To Unlock Your Potential: When you feel hassled or upset by the turns in the maze, ask yourself what is really bothering you about the situation. Allow no excuses, pinpoint whether you are angry with yourself, angry with someone else or if you may be feeling hopeless. Now, honestly evaluate what your options are to change or improve the situation. Consider all the options, even if some seem unreasonable. The goal this week is not to accept the way things are but to honestly evaluate how you would like things to be.

Chapter 6

Learn to say NO –
put YOU first sometimes

IT IS OK TO SAY NO! I REPEAT: IT IS OK TO SAY NO! This one change can free you from many obligations that you never wanted, never meant to accept or never thought would become lifelong commitments. This one change can mean the difference between doing what you want to do with your life and doing what others want you to do so they have more time to do what they want! This one change, if you choose to implement it, can help you find the time and courage to pursue other keys to unlocking your true potential! If you give away the finite level of energy you have, you won't be able to achieve your dreams.

When you finally gather the courage to say no, there will always be someone who will try to make you feel guilty for your decision. (More on this in Chapter 29) You deserve to reclaim your own power by saying no to others and yes to you. If you believe that your life is already being filled with non-negotiable obligations, it may be a signal that you are becoming lost or trapped in the maze.

This Week's Key To Unlock Your Potential: Take time to honestly evaluate what a "non-negotiable" obligation means to you. Think of a recent situation when you said yes but would have preferred to say no. Looking back, was there a way you could have graciously declined? Prepare a sentence that allows you to comfortably say no. For example, "I am sorry I can't help but I already dedicate five hours a week to volunteer service." Practice your well thought-out sentence next time you feel compelled to put another's needs before your own.

Chapter 7

Don't settle for less

This is a biggie. Set your standards high and relentlessly pursue what you desire. Not settling for less means...

- 🔳 Having the self-resolve to say, "I will wait for what I know I deserve."

- 🔳 Putting your best effort into all that you do and trusting that you will achieve greatness in your own way.

It does NOT mean...

- 🔳 Settling for nothing less than your neighbor has acquired.

- 🔳 Settling for nothing less than what your spouse/ significant other has determined is best for both of you.

🔲 Settling for nothing less than what your family raised you to achieve.

This is a very personal key. Measuring your standards on a bar set by others means permanently installing yourself on a treadmill of your own making. Have the courage to determine what *you* want out of life and make a promise to yourself that you will not settle for less.

This Week's Key To Unlock Your Potential: Look at your spouse/significant other, children, friends, house, car, job, clothes and vacation destinations and ask yourself if you are making choices based on personal likes and dislikes or if your decisions revolve around a desire to impress others. Write about a decision you made to impress someone else and how that choice made you feel. Then, write about a decision you made just for you and how that choice made you feel. The next time you want to give up on something important or find yourself struggling to keep up with someone else, re-read what you just wrote and settle for nothing less than what is best for YOU.

Chapter 8
Learn how to negotiate

There is a term in sales called ABC, which stands for "Always Be Closing." What it really comes down to in everyday life is to know ahead of time what you want and to always be looking for a way to get what you want out of every situation. I am not suggesting that you take advantage of every person or situation you encounter. Just remember that you are your own best asset. Every individual has unique traits that cannot be found in others. Learn what you do best and learn how to express to others what you do best. (More on this in Chapter 25) Also, (and this ties in with the previous chapter), learn how to say that you deserve more than the offer on the table.

For example, if you are at a customer service desk with a problem and the clerk isn't offering you a solution that you believe to be fair, here are three steps to follow: 1) simply state that you are not satisfied and why, 2) that you would like another option or to speak with someone who can provide another option, and 3) that you will not agree to settle the matter until you believe the solution is reasonable. Negotiating means not accepting the first offer but creating a solution that fits your needs without alienating the other party.

This Week's Key To Unlock Your Potential: Read at least one news story, magazine article, Web site or book about negotiating. Write down a negotiating tip that you can apply to your next customer service issue, purchase decision or career change and make a commitment to yourself to get more of what you want from the situation.

Chapter 9

Express gratitude for your mistakes and accomplishments

Most of the mistakes we make end up leading us to our greatest accomplishments. Be thankful for your mistakes; choose to see them as opportunities to improve your life. A mistake is often a door that opens on a new direction. Accomplishments may *appear* to be easy to be thankful for, but when was the last time you took a moment to inventory all the things that make you proud of who you are?

This Week's Key To Unlock Your Potential:
Write down a list of mistakes you have made and follow each mistake with the lesson you learned from the experience. Write down a list of your

accomplishments and follow each accomplishment with one reason you are grateful for the experience.

Chapter 10

Thank people –
Thank-you notes are even better!

Everyone leads busy lives. In our high tech, often impersonal society, people remember those who add a personal touch to their day. Someone who does something nice for you or has gone above and beyond what his or her job requires deserves a genuine thank-you. Think of a time that you have done a little something extra and found yourself muttering, "They didn't even have the decency to say thank you." What about the time you sent a special gift to someone out of town and never even received a note that said, "Thank you. The gift arrived and it was just what I wanted."

I am not suggesting that you should do nice things for others with the hope that they will recognize your generosity. Many kind acts do go unnoticed, but your note can add joy to another person's day. The reward of hand-writing a personalized thank-you note is that it helps you focus on the things in your life that you have to be grateful for.

In my experience, thank-you notes are even less common in business relationships. It's a quick, thoughtful way to show clients how important they are to you. An added benefit of business thank-you notes is that the receiver of that note will probably remember your gratitude long after the words have been expressed.

My younger sister gave me the thank-you note I treasure the most. Bernadine was always slightly shy and didn't want to leave home after community college to attend a four-year university to complete her degree in photography, her passion. I assured her I would be only a phone call away and that things would be fine if she just mustered up the courage to try. When she finally earned the degree, her thank-you note to me read, "To my wonderful sister, just want to thank you for all your support –emotional and financial! I am glad I went to college. Thanks again. Love, Bernadine." This note lingers in my memory and has a special place in my "feel good" folder (More on this in Chapter 45) because I never knew just how much my encouragement helped Bernadine find the strength to proceed along her chosen path.

This Week's Key To Unlock Your Potential: Express your gratitude and add joy to someone else's day by sending a personalized, handwritten thank-you note to one person each day of this week (don't cheat; there are seven days of the week to be thankful!)

Chapter 11

Explore your surroundings

Exploring your surroundings means looking at the things you pass by every day and seeing them in a new light. By looking for the subtle differences in familiar settings, you will learn to see how nothing remains the same, and that some changes are even better than you could have ever imagined.

Whenever I travel on business, I find a local deli or coffee shop (or in some small towns, the restaurant where locals gather for coffee) and talk to the people working there about what it's like to live in that particular corner of the world. I have the happiest memories and brightest stories from these escapades. What I have also found is that I often know more about what the area has to offer by a quick scan of the travel brochures than those who have spent their entire lives there and never noticed the riches of the scenery right in their own backyards.

This Week's Key To Unlock Your Potential:
Call your local chamber of commerce or visit their Web site and use this week to view your neighborhood through the eyes of a tourist. Think about what would make you want to relocate to your area if you were from somewhere else. Visit at least one museum, art exhibit, concert, park or nearby town. This will give you a new perspective about what your locale has to offer.

Chapter 12

Don't quit – Try, try again

Giving up is the easiest thing in the world to do. It takes great courage to keep trying when things don't seem to be going the way you had hoped. Review your progress, make changes where needed and learn from your mistakes, but don't quit just because something seems too hard.

My mom's favorite story to read to me when I was growing up was "The Little Engine That Could" by Watty Piper. It's the story of the small train that didn't think it could make it to the top of the mountain with a heavy load. But with each chug the little engine repeated, "I think I can," and as the engine finally crests the top of the mountain the chug becomes, "I thought I could!'" This is far more than a children's story; it's a lesson into adulthood: There are many challenges that can be overcome with just a positive attitude and a little determination.

This Week's Key To Unlock Your Potential:
Think about a situation you are facing that is not
advancing as smoothly as you would like. It may
be a relationship, project, business matter, health
issue or something else. Write down all the reasons
you would like to give up or end the struggle. Now,
try to turn each negative statement into something
positive. For the issues that seem doomed to failure,
list all of the options you have for improvements
and (if this is a path you still want to follow) vow
to try your best just once more.

Chapter 13

Keep your word

Your word is your reputation. Any promise made and not delivered makes it easier to break your word the next time around. It also creates a certain level of mistrust in the relationship between you and the other party involved. There are times when circumstances beyond your control will make it impossible to keep your word, but how you handle those times can help set you apart from the crowd. When you find it impossible to keep your word, take the time to apologize and explain what is preventing you from holding to the original agreement. You'll be surprised by how willing others are to help when they know the value of your promises.

My husband and I have an agreement that birthdays and anniversaries come before business. This is not to say there won't be some occasions when we will decide to celebrate on a different day, but what it does mean is that if something BIG happens to land on those days, we have agreed to decide *together* how to handle the situation. We might decide that we will travel together for business that week, or that one of us will take a day off to accommodate the other's schedule, but the point is that we include each other in those decisions. We've found that by keeping our word to each other in this area (and others), we have been better able to juggle the demands of our work.

This Week's Key To Unlock Your Potential:
Do you consider yourself to be a person who keeps his or her word? Pay attention to others you encounter throughout this week and determine who you can count on to always keep their word versus those who don't deliver on promises made. Commit to keeping your word and write about your observations. Note: You may discover that it is easier for you to say "no" (as discussed in Chapter 6) when you regard each of your promises as an obligation to keep your word.

Chapter 14

Choose your battles wisely

Ah, one of my hardest life lessons! I have to remind myself daily that I cannot fight the world. If you are a natural fighter, try to ask, "What outcome do I hope to reach by taking on this fight?" "What would my options be if I lost or chose not to fight?" And if you think something's worth fighting for but find confrontation difficult, try to ask, "Am I selling myself short just to avoid an uncomfortable situation?"

I have seen many people insist on avoiding all confrontation only to eventually explode at the worst possible moment — usually over something irrelevant — which just reinforces their belief that fighting will only make matters worse. The middle ground between confrontation and accommodation can often be achieved by approaching each situation as an opportunity for the needs of all to be met as opposed to a battle that only one will win.

What happens when we decide to hold all of our frustrations inside our bodies? We create an internal stress response! Karen Rosasco, APRN, BC, a family nurse practitioner at the Wege Institute for Mind Body and Spirit at St. Mary's Mercy Medical Center in Grand Rapids, Michigan, says she has seen many health conditions aggravated by stress. "Learning to recognize our stressors and successfully managing them is one of the best things we can do for ourselves," she advises.

Our bodies are very well equipped to adapt to an internal stress response, Rosasco said. Initially, the body responds to stress by increasing heart rate, blood pressure and body temperature. The strength and frequency of the heart rate increases, the arteries in our heart and skeletal muscles dilate, we use more oxygen and the smooth muscles of our gut relax.

"When this response is activated we release hormones that are designed to provide quick energy to the body," she said. "This is a great response short-term: the 'fight or flight' response. It is designed to give us the energy to either 'fight' our stress, or 'flee' from it."

In the long term, however, other mechanisms are needed to continue to provide the body with the energy it needs, and this can have very detrimental effects on our health. All our body systems are affected by stress. Prolonged stress can lead to common complaints such as muscle tension, stiffness and pain. It can also affect our digestive system, leading to feelings of nausea, bloating, cramping and constipation. Stress also contributes to the development of ulcers, colitis and irritable bowel syndrome. Our immune system also suffers, as stress suppresses the immune response and can result in frequent infections, allergies and chronic fatigue syndrome. Long-term stress can also lead to high blood pressure, heart attack, stroke and coronary artery disease.

Keeping a journal of stressors, Rosasco advises, can be an important tool in helping to develop better coping strategies.

I, for example, was born a fighter. My dad is a fighter; he comes from a family of fighters. I don't look for fights; in fact, I try to avoid *unnecessary* fights, but I have never backed down from an injustice that I had the ability to prevent. On the other hand, my mom and sister prefer to avoid confrontation unless it comes to self-defense or defending someone they love. This has taught me two things: 1) I cannot personally prevent all injustices, and 2) By focusing my energy on the things I can really change, I free up energy to achieve those things in life that are attainable without a fight.

*This Week's Key To Unlock Your Potential:
Determine whether you are fighting your way
through everything or whether you are avoiding
confrontation to such an extent that your life has
become too complacent. Do you need to back down
from some battles, or do you need to stand up and
fight for what you believe? Even if you think you
embody just the right amount of fight versus flight,
take a moment to write down the things in your life
that are worth fighting for.*

Chapter 15

Improve – EVERY DAY!

The first choice you are faced with every morning is whether or not you will make today better than yesterday. All of us have the choice to continually improve our lives (or reduce the number of dead ends in the maze). Just think what you can accomplish if you set your mind to learn or implement one new thing every day. If you think in terms of a goal you would like to meet and break it into simple steps, you can do anything.

I struggle to speak fluent Spanish (and look forward to also becoming fluent in Italian and French). I bought a calendar that exposes me to one new word in Spanish every day and has helped build my vocabulary, slowly and steadily. Although I still can't say that I'm fluent, I do know that I am one word wiser, one day at a time.

This Week's Key To Unlock Your Potential:
Write down every day of this week and after the
day write one thing you would like to improve. No
task is too small as long as you adopt the habit of
improvement.

Chapter 16

Be passionate

Have you ever noticed how a person who is exceptional at what he or she does always expresses a deep love of the apparent gift? Love life. Lose track of time. Get caught up in the moment. Choose to be not only present but truly, utterly involved in the things you do. Sing, laugh, dance and play. Life really is too short to not participate passionately in every moment.

People often tell me, "But I don't know what I really want." There are many books that suggest that passions lie somewhere in the activities you would do even if you weren't being paid to do them. Another signal of passion may be the activities that allow you to lose track of time. These theories may help you pinpoint certain interests, but I ask that you go one step further.

I believe that passion can be expressed even during those times you would rather be doing something else.

Not every hobby or interest will become your sole means of support, nor should it unless you determine that pursuing that path is what's ultimately right for you. I believe being passionate means embracing the good and bad in a situation. Sometimes the things we passionately dislike fuel an inner drive to make drastic change.

My husband is passionate about historic facts and monuments. I am not as interested in history but love to learn new things. Therefore, when we travel together and visit notable places, he focuses on the historic significance and I focus on how this experience may apply to current events. By slightly shifting my perspective, I am able to become passionately involved in the moment.

This Week's Key To Unlock Your Potential:
View each situation you encounter this week as an opportunity to live passionately in the moment. Even when things seem to be going "wrong," look for the gem in each experience. Document some of the moments that stand out in your mind, either good or bad, and notice how your attitude affected the outcomes.

Chapter 17

Build confidence

Is confidence an inborn or an acquired quality? I believe the answer is both. Confidence is something every person is born with the potential for, but sometimes events in childhood erode our natural confidence. And sometimes the most confident child experiences something in adulthood that strips away the confidence that was built. In order to stay confident, we must practice being confident. Successes, failures, obstacles, opportunities and everyday events provide an arena to build confidence. The easiest way to be confident is to believe in what you say and do.

One of my great honors was an invitation to sit on a "Building Confidence Panel" at the local Women's Resource Center. As a guest panelist, I met three other women from very different life paths who each shared a story of triumph against the odds in some area of life.

41

The women in the audience were of all ages, races, economic levels and professions. I was there to share my ideas about how women can gain confidence, but walked away with the knowledge that confidence comes in as many forms as there are people. Only when we are willing to face our fears, learn from our own circumstances and to continually build each day upon the confidence that we already have will we earn the reward of greater confidence. (More on this in Chapters 30 and 34)

This Week's Key To Unlock Your Potential:
Write a couple of sentences about what confidence means to you. Now conjure up an image of the most confident person you know and add any other ideas about confidence that come to mind. Write about how having more confidence could change your outlook on life and choose three things you will do this week to boost your confidence.

Chapter 18

Notice coincidence

    I believe that coincidence and déjà vu' are signs we are on the right path. When you find yourself thinking, "What a coincidence!" pay very close attention to what happens next, because you might discover a message in the experience. The more frequently you encounter a feeling that what you are about to experience has happened before, the closer you are to your true path — so look closely for clues to your next step. For example, if something happens in threes, make it your responsibility to follow up. Let's imagine you hear the name of a friend you haven't spoken to in a while. Maybe later the same night you have a dream about that person, and the next day while looking through your address book for a business contact you come across his or her business card. (More on coincidence in dreams in Chapter 20) This would be an excellent time to give this friend a call to catch up on each other's lives. You never know, you may just find the answer to a problem that has had you losing sleep or hear about a job opening that would inspire you to pursue that long-forgotten desire.

I look for coincidence in everything I do, in every person I encounter and especially in nature. My special coincidence symbol is a cardinal. My paternal grandmother, Grandma Florence Carey, died when I was 16 years old. My uncle, her son, was preparing a eulogy to present at the church service and decided he would like to talk about how Grandma loved cardinals. He wanted to remind all of us how every day Grandma would gaze out the window into her postage stamp-sized backyard and watch the birdbath for a visit from "her" cardinals. No matter how many tribulations her life held, the cardinals always brought her joy.

Well, as my uncle walked with his family to the funeral home just a few blocks from Grandma's house, he was thinking about the story he was about to tell when a cardinal landed on a tree branch alongside the sidewalk and began to sing. All of them watched in awe as the cardinal happily bounced from tree to tree singing a beautiful melody on that gloomy, drizzly April day. As my uncle relayed the story, there was not a dry eye in the church. His initial idea of asking us to think about Grandma whenever a cardinal was spotted took on new meaning for all of us.

This happened back in 1990, but to this day when I see a cardinal I know I am on the right path and that things will be ok. For instance, when I was passed over for a scholarship I was depending on in order to complete my four-year degree, I "coincidentally" saw and heard a cardinal singing on a branch outside a classroom window, only to have an even better scholarship awarded shortly after. My father saw a cardinal outside the window of his doctor's office as he waited for test results that had all of us very worried; the results, as it turned out, were normal. And my sister was "visited" by a cardinal that landed on a tree in her yard and began to sing as she moved into her first new home. Coincidence? You decide.

This Week's Key To Unlock Your Potential: Pay attention to subtle messages that you encounter. You may hear yourself or someone else say, "what a coincidence." You may suddenly think of a person then see them or receive their call, or experience a sense of having done something before. Think about how this "coincidence" may hold an answer to a question or dilemma you currently face. Jot down notes about each occurrence and decide for yourself whether or not you believe that there are no coincidences.

Chapter 19

Pay attention to what YOU want out of life

Ask yourself, "If I could do ANYTHING, what would it be?" You may already know what you want but you may have yourself convinced that you will have to make too many sacrifices, or give up too much of what you already have to get to where you would rather be. When you notice all the times in your life when you experience joy, happiness, and even dissatisfaction, you're catching glimpses of your purpose. If you really don't know your purpose in life, pay attention to what you already know about yourself and try new things until you find a path that you can't imagine not pursuing.

I believe the key to finding the pattern to what YOU want the most can be discovered by making a list of the things in your life that evoke the most passion. (As discussed in Chapter 16) Though this book provides a place to start your inventory, I encourage you to keep an ongoing journal so you can look back over your progress. Through the goals at the end of each chapter, I present ideas to help you get in touch with where you are now. My intention is that by the time you reach the book's conclusion you will see a pattern that points to what you want out of life.

This Week's Key To Unlock Your Potential: Create a list of things that you are passionate about; remember, it should include things you passionately like and things you passionately dislike! Add to this list throughout the week as you encounter a variety of people and situations.

Chapter 20

Record your dreams

Not everyone believes in the power of dreams. Some people even deny that they dream at all. But sleeping an average of eight hours a night equals one-third of your lifetime. So if you remember your dreams and believe in their power, you may want to add dreams to your journal. Learning key dream symbol interpretation may help you as you continue to unlock your potential. There are many books on this subject; my favorite is "The Dream Book: Symbols for Self-Understanding" by Betty Bethards.

"Dreams help you see yourself as you are: your true inner beauty, your potential, where you are both missing and getting the point of lessons you are working on. Nothing is more important than to know yourself. This makes all things on all planes in all realities easy." Bethards, p.52

"Everything has its own significance. Fences or road blocks indicate that creative thinking is needed to get beyond a particular problem that is now facing you. The kind of road on which you find yourself traveling represents how smooth or rough your journey is at present. If you are on a freeway it is easy going. If a bumpy road you are getting there but it is a little rough at present. If you are paving a road you are making your way easier for the future." Bethards, p.39

"Any symbol given to you – whether in fantasy, meditation or guided imagery – are all the same. They are coded messages from self to self. When you 'get the picture,' you understand the situation." Bethards, p.39

"You Are The Final Word"
"Remember that you are always your own best interpreter. You are the final word on the meaning of a symbol for you." Bethards, p.40

In Chapter 18: Notice Coincidence, I suggested that you pay attention to dreams about conversations with people you know, or people you haven't seen or thought of in a long time. When I dream of someone I make a habit of calling that person to say he or she is on my mind. I consider these "reminder dreams," because they usually occur when I've gotten too busy racing around to stay in touch. On occasion, I have conversations in my dreams with people I've encountered in my waking life.

These "dream" conversations have often provided answers to questions or led to new opportunities. I sometimes wonder how altered my life path would be if I dismissed these reminders and messages as "just dreams."

This Week's Key To Unlock Your Potential: Before you go to sleep each night this week tell yourself you would like to remember a dream when you awaken. Write down all the details that you can remember and go to the library or a bookstore to look up what the dream symbols may be trying to tell you. Dream interpretation is very personal, so you may choose to start with a household dictionary to explore the meaning of dream symbols. Relax; even if you don't believe in the power of dreams, this can be a simple way to add a little fun to your day.

Rat Race Relaxer ————————————————

Chapter 21

Develop a list of everything you have ever wanted to do

It is important to write down everything you want to do, no matter how big or how small. WHY is a list so important?

- ✍ You can't devise a solid plan to do the things you hope to do until you know what all of those things are.

- ✍ Creating a list sets your intention to accomplish the things that you perceive to be the most essential. (More on this in Chapter 31)

- ✍ A list provides a deliberate space to add new items as they become significant.

- ✍ The act of crossing items off the list as they are achieved can be very rewarding.

My own list includes everything from spending at least 10 minutes a day in silent meditation to appearing on *The Oprah Show*™.

This Week's Key To Unlock Your Potential: Write down your list of everything you have ever wanted to do. Revisit this list often as you work through the upcoming chapters (and beyond) and discover new interests and goals. This list is never complete; it is endless.

Chapter 22

Write down your wishes and hopes

Wishes and hopes will complement the section you just completed about all the things you would like to do. Sometimes it is easier to let your mind wander when you focus on hopes and wishes because they can be less intimidating or overwhelming than the action required in a to-do list. For example, " I wish I knew what I wanted to do with my life" is easier to say than "I challenge myself to do at least one thing each day to create the life I want to live."

This Week's Key To Unlock Your Potential:
Write out your list of hopes and wishes. Even include things that you have no intention of actually pursuing. The point is to generate an exhaustive list of everything and anything you would love to

do if there were no boundaries and limitless opportunity. After your hopes and wishes list is complete, you may want to turn certain wishes into actionable steps and add them to your to-do list from the previous chapter.

Chapter 23

Write down the things that make you angry

Anger is very personal; what angers you may not anger someone else. It doesn't matter whether you are angry with yourself, someone else or the situation you are facing because you are the only one who has the power to come to terms with your anger. For example, if you express anger toward someone else and that person apologizes, you are left with a decision of releasing or holding on to the anger. But the same is true if the other person refuses to apologize, because you still hold the internal formula for offering forgiveness or holding a grudge.

Anger can be a destructive force that when left unchecked may consume your thoughts and actions and hold you to a person or event that happened far in the past. Like stress, anger can also affect your health and mental well-being. By effectively managing your anger, you can use the energy it generates to propel you forward. One way to free up energy for more constructive changes is to write down things that anger you. When you see your angers on paper you can make the choice to remain angry or to practice forgiveness.

I've learned to ask myself why I'm angry, what I can do to change the situation and how I can move beyond my anger when I've done all that I can do. Now when I take the time to write about something that angers me, I usually feel energized afterward because it takes more exertion for me to contain the anger than it does to analyze and release it.

This Week's Key To Unlock Your Potential: Write down everything that you can think of that makes you angry. Don't hold back; use the paper as a punching bag for anyone and anything that irritates or infuriates you. When you finally stop, force yourself to write some more — go ahead, write about how angry you get when you have to keep making lists! Feel better? Now look at each item and make reasoned, proactive choices as you move toward the future: is there something you can do to end your anger, are there certain people/events worth holding a grudge against, or should some of these situations be forgiven and left in the past?

Chapter 24
Write down your fears

Face your fears! Take away *their* power over *your* actions and emotions. When you're able to look at all of your fears in the form of a list, it makes them appear more manageable than they appear in your mind's eye. Writing down your fears can release an overwhelming amount of energy, but actually taking small steps to conquer each fear can mean the difference between success and failure.

I feel like a huge weight has been lifted from me whenever I write down my fears. Whenever I am afraid to take the next step, I take a deep breath and force myself to press on just a little further. As far back as I can remember, my dad always encouraged me to face my fears. I was the first grandchild on both sides of my parents' families, so the running joke was that my dad's family would tell me, "You're Irish," and my mom's family would tell me, "You're Italian." When I was about three years old, I was terrified of Santa Claus. I did not like beards, I did not want to sit on "stranger danger's" lap, and I did not want my picture taken with someone who was just a stand-in, not the "real" thing. This turned into a battle at the mall, because, like all proud moms, my mom really wanted to have "little JoAnna's" picture taken with Santa. I started to cry — probably to get my own way, but also because I was just so afraid that this guy in the red suit would steal me away from my mom and dad. This is where my dad stepped in and with a little trickery said, "If you're too afraid to have your picture taken with Santa, then you're not tough and you're not Irish." Since I've always been a daddy's girl, I had to prove that day that I was Irish. I swallowed hard, choked back those tears and marched myself right up to have that picture taken. It might not have been the gentlest way to talk me into having that picture taken, but it taught me a valuable lesson: Even though my eyes may grow as big as saucers when faced with something I fear, I do have the strength in me to take a deep breath and march forward.

This Week's Key To Unlock Your Potential: Write down an exhaustive list of your fears. Pay attention to subtle physical reactions as you go through each day; are you afraid of not being smart or attractive enough, of asking questions, or of new surroundings? This week, don't just write about your fears; tackle one small step each day to overcome some of those fearful items that block your potential. Keep adding to this list as you continue through the Rat Race Relaxer because it isn't always easy to admit your fears, much less put them into words.

Chapter 25

Create an inventory list of all past jobs and skills learned

What do you know? What do you do better than others? It doesn't matter whether you have acquired skills through school, jobs, being a parent or just living life every day, you have something special to contribute to the world. Maybe you were born mechanically inclined, or with a beautiful singing voice, an athletic ability or a gift for dealing effectively with people. YOU ARE GREAT AT SOMETHING!

Some people try to take the easy way out by saying they have no skills, abilities or gifts. Don't be modest on this list. Write down everything you can think of that you are wonderful at. No excuses. If you have ever whined, "What do I know?" choose to be confident today. If you're great at quilting, write it down. If you know how to throw a spectacular party, write it down. Even if the only thing in this world you know how to do is make people laugh, write that down and I know your other skills will flood into your mind. This list will help you decide which of your skills you would like to further develop and may even uncover other skills you wish to acquire.

This Week's Key To Unlock Your Potential: Create an inventory list of all your past jobs and skills learned. This list should include job skills, life skills, hobbies, etc., so it fully reflects your unique personality. This list can be added to the "feel-good" folder (developed in Chapter 45) to remind you of all the skills and abilities that make you exceptional.

Chapter 26

Identify the best thing that's ever happened in your life and the best job you've ever had

What brings you joy? What are your fondest memories? Think about the events in your life that you believe to have been the high points of your journey. Then think specifically about the jobs you've had that still make you smile. What were the skills needed and duties involved that you found so enjoyable?

When I was taking an inventory of the best times in my job history, I kept thinking about the coffeehouse I worked in after college while I interviewed for marketing positions. I loved talking to the customers, teaching them about the different drinks, hearing their stories. Thinking about what I liked about each of my past jobs helped me rediscover a goal I had set while I was in college of building my own business. I began my career with a goal of gaining on-the-job experience and finding something I loved to do. What I eventually earned were the skills and confidence I needed to build my own business in my own way. But it wasn't until I looked back upon my best moments that my new path became clear.

This Week's Key To Unlock Your Potential: Identify the best thing that's ever happened in your life and the best job you've ever had. Describe in detail what was great about these events. Did you encounter obstacles while you were racing toward these moments, or did they simply happen? What lessons did you learn during these good times? To keep the "rat race" in focus, take a moment to list any NEGATIVE outcomes of events that you initially perceived as positive.

Chapter 27

Identify the worst thing that's ever happened in your life and the worst job you've ever had

Did I fail when I opted out of my corporate job, or did I succeed in starting my own business? I choose to see the major events in my life as catalysts for where I was meant to soar in the future.

Overturn your failures! Life is a matter of perspective. When you think about the worst thing that has ever happened in your life and job, consider that failing to complete one path means the opportunity to have the courage to start something new. Have you failed in a relationship only to rediscover yourself or a new partner who brings you more joy? Have you failed at one job only to go on to learn new skills and build upon your experience? Grant yourself the same leniency as you review your past that you would grant a friend.

This Week's Key To Unlock Your Potential: Identify the worst thing that's ever happened in your life and the worst job you've ever had. Describe in detail what was so unpleasant about these events. Could you have prevented these moments, or did they simply happen? What lessons did you learn during these bad times? To keep the "rat race" in focus, take a moment to list any POSITIVE outcomes of events that you initially perceived as negative.

Chapter 28

List the people in your life who aid your progress

All of us have certain people in our lives who are always there to share triumphs and failures, to roar a supportive battle cry when things get tough, to lend strength when we are too weak to stand alone, or to just listen when we need a friend. I believe it's our duty to surround ourselves with those who aid in our development and to provide the same kind of environment for those who seek the support of our unique gifts. Make the intention to surround yourself with others who will help you and watch the list of supporters grow. (More on this in Chapter 34)

Start a support network. Begin with an informal phone call or visit to someone in your life who has always been there for you. Thank them for believing in you and encourage them to share their hopes, fears, joys and sadness so you can also be there for them. This will allow the relationship to grow in a way that helps each of you face life's challenges. The key is not to dwell only on good experiences or only on bad experiences, but to acknowledge the beauty in all and enjoy the strength that others can provide. Eventually, you may decide to set aside an informal group of your closest supporters to share their stories. A great way to meet new people is to share your mission/ideas (More on this in Chapter 31) and ask those you know for referrals to others who might be able to support you.

This Week's Key To Unlock Your Potential:
Write down the name of every person who has helped you on your journey. They can be from the past or present, living or passed on. Think of the gifts bestowed by each of these people and determine what gifts you would like to attract into your life right now. To take this key one step further, make an informal phone call to one of your supporters and explain the "support network" idea from this chapter so you can help each other navigate this "rat race maze."

Chapter 29

Identify the people in your life who block your progress

Don't share your feelings with people who undermine what you do or say. Don't share your thoughts with people who always make you feel worse than you did before you spoke. Learn to separate yourself from those who sap your power and leave you feeling tired and discouraged.

Often the people closest to us forget to respect our independent points of view. Disrespect may be disguised as negativity, condescension, discouragement, belittlement, pessimism, disapproval, ridicule, mockery or even abuse. Demonstrate your confidence and self-respect by explaining to others when their behavior becomes hurtful and unacceptable. In order to unlock your full potential, you must make a promise to yourself to limit the time you spend with people who will not respect your feelings. You are the owner of your thoughts! Consider before you speak that you may be sabotaging your own progress by sharing your innermost thoughts with others before you are ready for the repercussions of disapproval.

I can just hear you asking, "What if the person who brings the most negativity is a spouse, a child or someone else so close that he or she cannot be avoided?" My answer is to always begin by trying to include the people closest to you in your journey. Sometimes you have to guard your feelings, thoughts and ideas as you would guard a child. Notice I did not say to hide these feelings, but to only discuss things when you are confident enough to explain your decisions. You may have to continually remind yourself and others that you are responsible for your own happiness. Ultimately, you may decide that you are settling for less than you deserve by allowing unsupportive people to hinder your decisions. At the end of the Rat Race Relaxer you will find a list of suggested readings if you're interested in further discussion of this topic, but only you can decide when enough is enough.

This Week's Key To Unlock Your Potential:
Write down the names of every person who may be
blocking your progress by causing you pain or

depleting your energy. After each name, describe in detail the behaviors that are affecting you and how the behaviors make you feel. Is there a common theme among these detractors? What can you do to protect yourself from these people and situations? Are any of the relationships so painful that it is time for you to say "Enough!" and find the courage to move on?

Chapter 30

Track your journey – Whom have I met? What have I learned?

People make the world go around. You may have heard the term "six degrees of separation" – meaning that you are only six people away from knowing anyone in the world. This theory is still being tested to determine whether we are truly that connected to one another, but if you talk to someone at length you will often find some connection, someone whom each of you know. This is why networking is such a sought-after skill. When you become great at networking, others want to know your secret.

I keep an ongoing list of every person I meet on my journey. When someone refers me to another contact, I list that person below the referral's name. I sometimes add ideas that the contact has inspired or items we discussed that I would like to follow up on. It's amazing how the lists begin to merge. It's always interesting to look back and see the people-connections between new opportunities.

This Week's Key To Unlock Your Potential:
Begin to keep a list of the people you meet on your journey. When someone refers you to another person, add the name of the referral source as well as the new contact to the list. Develop a habit of asking these new contacts for the names of others who may be able to help you. Keep track of what you learn or ideas generated through these meetings and, as you discovered in Chapter 18, you may "notice coincidence."

Chapter 31

Make your mission/ideas foremost in your mind

Know where you are headed so when you see an opportunity that will help you reach your goals, you'll be in the best position to take that next step. All the lists and inventories I have asked you to create — who you are, what you would like to do, your hopes, fears and wishes — allow you to create a life mission. If you don't feel confident enough to create a mission, start with a group of goals you would like to accomplish over the next year. Keep experimenting until you find an idea that you believe you were meant to relentlessly pursue. Remember, it is your mission and it can change as you grow and excel; you are the only limit to what you can become.

Imagine that a genie were to grant you three wishes. If all you can come up with is, "I would like to be rich and thin," you haven't taken enough time to know your true goals. Ask yourself what you would DO if you were rich and thin and you will see a hint of your true mission. Now ask yourself if any of the things you named are things you can do right now and, if so, why you choose not to follow through.

This Week's Key To Unlock Your Potential:
Read over all of the lists you have created to this point and consider how this documentation process has affected the way you approach people, events and daily risks. Use the information to create your life mission statement. Don't be intimidated; just write down whatever pops into your head as you read your own story. It can be as ambitious or as simplistic as you desire, and it is ever-changing. You can start with a few things you want to change, ideas you want to pursue, people you want to meet, or a new hobby you want to try. Then, when you see an opportunity that will help you reach your goal, you'll be in the best position to take that next step. Your life mission should merely identify your aspirations and serve as a roadmap as you navigate the maze.

Chapter 32

Track your progress

Most of us have probably heard the popular saying, "If you don't know where you have been, you won't know where you are going." It is important to set attainable goals and celebrate every small victory. Even if you take one sheet of paper and write just three things you would like to do in the next year, make sure you cross off each one as you go along. This is addictive! Once you see how easy it is to accomplish things when you make an intention, you'll want the satisfaction of going back over your notes just to see all of the things you've finally done that you had always promised to make time to do.

Diplomas, degrees, training and certifications are examples of goals that provide an end product that allows us to track our progress. Every time we pass a grade level, complete a class or attend a training seminar and receive a piece of paper that shows we had the perseverance to complete what we set out to accomplish, it gives us the courage to take the next step.

This Week's Key To Unlock Your Potential:
In the last chapter you identified your life mission, or at least a few ideas that you would like to pursue. Your challenge this week is to write down three or more concrete steps you can take to bring you closer to your mission. By the end of the week, complete at least one of these steps and cross it off the list. Your ongoing challenge is to relax into this step-by-step method of setting, reaching and crossing off goals that map out your journey through the maze. This process helps you live more in the moment by taking the main focus off of the future and placing your attention on what you can do right now.

Chapter 33

Practice courage

You can unlock reserves of potential by just mustering up the courage to try one small thing at a time that you would normally avoid with an excuse such as, "Oh, I am too afraid of heights to climb that ladder, and besides, I have never been the best at climbing." Even small steps make a big difference when you are committed to being courageous. You may be only two rungs higher on the ladder today than you were yesterday, but with constant practice you can be on top of the world.

Gregg, one of my mentors, practiced small steps of courage to overcome his fear of heights. He attributed this fear to an incident when he was just 10 months old. Gregg was in his stroller when his brother opened the accordion gate that was blocking the basement stairs and Gregg rolled to the bottom. Due to the severe blow to his head, Gregg was unconscious for the next five hours. In Gregg's opinion, this incident may have made his fear of heights more severe than the average person's.

During college, Gregg worked at Monsanto, the third largest chemical producer in the United States at that time. Outside of the factory, exposed to the elements, was a 140-foot tall equipment column that was about four feet in diameter. Along the outside of the tower, a ladder ascended 20 feet to the first platform, then another 20 feet of ladder up to the next platform, for a total of seven "flights". At the top of the tower was a huge cooling fan with a blade that looked like an airplane propeller. This fan generated 100 mile per hour winds and a deafening noise level. The trek to the top of the tower was frightening even to some of the workers who were not afraid of heights, but climbing that tower was something that Gregg decided he had to do if he wanted to conquer his fear.

"I was too afraid to go all the way up at first, so I just would go up a level or two, slowly increasing until I made it to the top over a period of weeks," Gregg recalled. "After that, I went up every day because it felt good to win, and to keep the terror from returning. I overcame this phobia by taking little steps of courage — it really works."

This Week's Key To Unlock Your Potential:
Look at the list of fears you created in Chapter 24
and choose one fear you would like to overcome.
Determine the steps of courage you can practice
throughout this week in an effort to conquer your
fear.

Rat Race Relaxer ——————————————

Chapter 34

Learn about the obstacles and accomplishments of others by reading, attending seminars and through personal contact

Living to your full potential is never easy; it means always being willing to stretch the boundaries of where you have been. Find inspiration in the stories of others. Learn how others have achieved what they consider to be successes or how they overcame great hurdles and you can find strength to continue your own path. Every one of us has a story to tell and most people are flattered that you would want to know what it is like to walk in their shoes.

I always love to hear stories of other women — especially those of past generations — to gain insight into how my life would have been different had I been born at another time. Often, no one else has ever asked them, "What was your life like? What would you have done differently?" I find that strangers share their life stories with me more easily than the women in my own family. But some of my fondest memories are when my 90-plus-year-old great-grandmother shares even the smallest details of what it was like when she was a girl, student, teenager, young woman, employee, wife and mother. My life is richer for all the words of wisdom that have been passed on during what others would believe to be idle conversation.

This Week's Key To Unlock Your Potential: Attend a seminar that attracts your attention, read an autobiography, or simply ask someone you consider interesting to share his or her story. This is not only a fun way to "relax," it also provides a moment of escape from your own race.

Chapter 35

Love others for who they ARE, not for who they can BE

Each one of us controls our own life and happiness. A loss of energy is inevitable if effort is dedicated to changing those around us instead of looking inward for the changes we seek. Instead of trying to convince others to change how they approach a situation, look for a value you would like to change in yourself. Loving others for who they are, in turn, allows you to accept yourself for being less than perfect. Create an environment of love for yourself and others and it will cultivate further growth.

This Week's Key To Unlock Your Potential: In the rat race, we all encounter people whose actions ultimately undermine progress. This week, ask yourself what you have to learn from the people in your life. Instead of trying to overcome differences that have been causing strife, identify at least one of your own qualities that you consider less than perfect. Use this week to embrace that quality as being something that makes you an original!

Chapter 36

Express YOUR opinion

Keep your own power. Your opinions are yours alone, and it's ok to express those opinions without guilt or shame. This is not to say you should believe your opinion is the only way of doing things or that you should express your opinion about every topic under the sun. But if you feel very strongly about something, be direct. It is better to say, "I have a different opinion" than to always bend your views to meet the needs of others. This can be tempered with Chapter 1: "Practice being open-minded" and Chapter 14: "Choose battles wisely."

When asked a question, do you often find yourself responding, "I don't know"? Often the phrase "I don't know" is simply an excuse for not wanting to express an opinion. Say you're heading out to dinner. Your dinner partner turns to you and asks, "What do you have a taste for tonight?" You've been craving Chinese food all day but you know your companion would prefer a meat and potatoes meal, so you casually answer, "Oh, I don't know, you decide." You knew exactly what you wanted, but were hesitant to just express your opinion. Why? Later, you may even find yourself arguing, "No one ever does what I want to do" or, "You never ask about my likes and dislikes." Don't fall into chronic dissatisfaction by continuing to avoid your true desires. People are not mind readers. Express your opinion. Start with the small things and work at building the confidence and bravery you need to move onto the items that can really change your life.

This Week's Key To Unlock Your Potential:
For one whole week resist the temptation to utter those three little words, "I don't know." Instead, chose to express your opinion. Document the reaction of others to your willingness to express an opinion and notice if there is any difference in the way you feel about yourself.

Chapter 37

*Stay true to yourself –
Practice your own set of principles
and be proud of what you stand for*

Take a stand! Harness the strength and courage you have worked so hard to build and determine what you stand for. Do you believe in freedom, joy, sadness, pain, fairness, loyalty, workmanship, or something else? Who are you? Are you still learning, or are you the same person you were ten years ago? Have you ever stood up for yourself and your ideals, even when you knew it would create tension, complications or a battle?

When confronted with change or a dilemma, are you able to determine what YOU believe about a situation, or do you always turn to friends, family, neighbors or the media? There may be no possible way to tune out all of this "noise" and have a wholly "pure" opinion, but notice

91

to what degree you are being influenced by the opinions of those around you. Feeling compelled to always have the radio on in the car, watch the news EVERY DAY, or habitually read news and entertainment magazines? Eliminating this clutter from your workspace and life is one way to de-stress, free up more time and minimize outside influences. Reducing these external influencers may help you relax more and race less. Eventually, the important hard news and celebrity gossip will make it your way without having to continually read, watch, study, debate and fill your brain with trivia.

I have been called idealistic, optimistic, realistic, a chameleon, a freedom fighter, aggressive, not aggressive enough, compassionate, not empathetic enough, funny and not so funny. The point is, labels used by others to describe me are sometimes true and sometimes false, but ultimately just individual perceptions. By knowing who I am and what I stand for, I am not persuaded much by the opinions of others. I might seek advice and implement ideas from others, but I make the final decisions regarding how to proceed on my journey based on where I have been and where I aspire to be. There have been times when I passed up a job opportunity or chose not to form partnerships with others due to conflicts of interest. But I believe that by staying true to my principles, I eventually create greater overall wealth.

This Week's Key To Unlock Your Potential: Reduce the external influencers. Spend time in the car without listening to the radio, vow not to watch the news every day, read fewer news and entertainment magazines. For one whole week stay true to yourself, rely on your own principles instead of input from others. Make this a week to relax more and race less.

Chapter 38

Incorporate the phrase
... "Tell me more" ...
into your conversations

These three words, "Tell me more," can open windows of opportunity and uncover surpluses of information. People love to talk about themselves and the things that matter most in their lives, be it family, business, hobbies, or travel. Just asking for more information can provide ideas for your next big project, a contact with a potential client, or the location of your dream vacation. Listen closely to the thoughts shared by others because those stories often contain lessons that help to unlock your true potential.

Morgan, a newspaper reporter, learned that the phrase "tell me more" works very well in her line of business. She says, "People often believe that they are too busy to be curious about others, but there is so much to be learned by interacting. I find that this is especially true when working with children because I can tap into my own long-lost childlike sense of curiosity." In Morgan's reporting experience, she says the real story is often not the one she initially thought she was covering.

This Week's Key To Unlock Your Potential: Incorporate the phrase "Tell Me More" into your conversations with others. Examples for using this phrase as an icebreaker with someone you've just met may include, "Tell me more about your hobbies, career, family, or favorite travels." Business uses may include, "Tell me more about upcoming projects, promotions, or expansion plans."

Chapter 39

Ask questions; listen in silence

The fastest way to learn something new is to ask questions. In my opinion, the fastest way to discredit what you are about to say is to preface your question with an apology for having to ask. Why? Because each time you ask a question it gives the person responding an opportunity to clarify his or her perspective. And what you have to say is just as important as the comments of anyone else in the room, so relinquish your need to apologize for asking questions.

Always ask as many questions as it takes until you fully understand. If you are afraid to ask questions, return to the list of fears you created in Chapter 24, add "asking questions" and overcome the fear!

Whenever you ask a question, it is essential to practice silence so the person has a chance to respond.

Many people are afraid to have a silent moment in conversation so they rush to fill the quiet space. Become comfortable with silence and it will give you an advantage in at least two ways. One, allowing a moment of silence after you ask a question sends a subtle, nonverbal clue that you are expecting an answer. Two, pausing after someone asks you a direct question allows a moment to gather your thoughts so you will be less likely to fill the air with non-words such as "uh" or "um."

3 Questions That Can Change Your Life

1. "Why?"

   Spend time with a child and you will realize how vital the question "Why?" is to learning. If you have stopped asking why, chances are that you are not stretching the boundaries of what you know, or have become so bogged down in the minutiae of your own life that you have lost the natural curiosity necessary for growth.

2. "What are my options?"

   This is especially helpful when you feel that a situation is beyond your control, such as when your employer offers you a new position that would require more travel than you'd like. When in doubt, asking for options may provide you with a solution you had not considered. This is an excellent time to practice silence. The question speaks for itself.

3. "Is there anything else I should know?"
   Top salespeople are trained to uncover crucial facts by asking the right questions. Use this question to uncover extra information and details in any situation. Most people, if asked this question at the end of a conversation, will add more details, and it is often information they would not provide during normal question and answer discovery.

This Week's Key To Unlock Your Potential:
Don't retrace your steps through the maze. Save time, effort and hours of rework by gaining clarification. Ask questions without apologizing for having to ask. Practice using silences when you ask a question and when a question is directed to you. When in doubt, don't guess; just ask!

Chapter 40

Right-size your life

Does your life as it stands make you happy? Are you overextended financially, emotionally, mentally, physically, or all of the above? Are there things in your life that you are attached to simply to buffer the pain of your unfulfilled desires? Is there a long list of things you would love to do – such as take a vacation, go back to school, exercise or sleep in more often – if only you had the time or money? Or are you rewarding yourself with BELONGINGS because you are stressed out or unhappy with life situations? Are you always keeping score by measuring what you have as compared with your significant other, family, friends, or neighbors? Maybe it's time to reflect upon your life and decide which areas of your life need growth and which areas you've outgrown.

This Week's Key To Unlock Your Potential:
Right-sizing your life is one of the key components
of forging a path that is custom-tailored to your
needs. If you think you are living beyond your
financial, physical, familial or spiritual needs,
consider some of the practical ways that you can
begin making necessary changes to your life. Look
at the family budget, talk to your employer about
flexible scheduling options, consider doing without
some luxury, or find a way to incorporate more
enjoyable activities into your days. This week is
about capturing an aerial view of what you have
been racing toward and choosing which of these
paths you will continue to explore.

Chapter 41

Take a vacation!

In a 2001 Harris Poll of 1,011 adults nationwide, the average time spent on work and school was 50 hours a week, versus 20 hours a week for leisure activities. Might sound reasonable, but compare those figures to the 41 hours a week for work and school and 26 hours a week for leisure activities cited in 1973. The trend is clear: we're taking less and less time for ourselves.

How long has it been since your last vacation? What are you waiting for? No time, no money, or poor health are common excuses for putting off a vacation, but there's no time like the present to discover how a vacation can provide a whole new outlook. Even if you have to adhere to a shoestring budget or start by taking a long weekend, make a promise to treat yourself (and maybe those closest to you) to the rejuvenation that a few days surrounded by new scenery can provide.

Travelers often list the following benefits of vacation: provides change of pace, lifts spirits, promotes learning, broadens horizons, increases cultural awareness, reduces stress and encourages rejuvenation.

The anticipation of a vacation will help me through even the most difficult days. Just the process of choosing the next adventure lifts my spirits and puts a smile on my face. Before I began traveling for public speaking I had visited 36 states, five Canadian cities and eight islands in the Southern Caribbean. Every trip inspired a greater appreciation for natural wonders, a better understanding of how people live and an insatiable wanderlust. Travel has opened my eyes to the beauty of variety; no two towns, cities, or islands are the same and yet so many places seem familiar, so many people share the same hopes, dreams and fears. Through exploring, I have found my place.

Many people don't think they have the money for vacations, even small ones. Morgan, the editor of this book, found a creative way to afford time away – "savings bottles." A "vacation" bottle started this creative savings strategy because Morgan just couldn't seem to set aside the money she needed for a trip to Toronto, Canada.

One payday, Morgan took an empty bottle and shoved a few dollars down the long, thin neck and vowed that with each paycheck she would add what she could spare to this vacation fund. Even though this money wasn't secured and gaining interest in a traditional savings account, it was a system that proved effective. By the time the date for the Toronto trip arrived, there was more than double the amount of cash needed for the initial goal. Morgan smiles as she tells me, "Happiness for me is having something to look forward to. When I put that bottle full of cash in a plastic bag and go outside to smash it open, there's something victorious and ritualistic about the process. Even now I'm amazed that I find the money to add to those bottles. The financial picture hasn't changed, just my focus." A six-pack of empty bottles now serves as Morgan's dream fund, with each bottle representing a goal or item she is working at attaining.

This Week's Key To Unlock Your Potential: Taking one small break from the high-speed race of life can help you find a fresh perspective. Vacation time helps you to recharge, replenish, rediscover your surroundings, and above all else, relax! Use this week to research and plan your next vacation. If you can't afford to venture far from home, simply plan to take a few days off, consider some of the ideas in this book for a more enjoyable life, or brainstorm ideas for low-cost, nearby activities (as discussed in Chapter 11). Find some way to set aside at least a few days to recharge.

Chapter 42

Ponder this saying:
Be a human being, not a human doing

Life has become so fast-paced that people are rushing from one thing to the next in order to fulfill obligations. In a rush to DO what is expected, we often neglect the things we would find more enjoyable. Try to take a few moments every day to just sit and BE. Use the time to think about where you have been, where you are going and how to live in the moment. If you find yourself saying, "I don't have time to sit and think; I have things to do," then it's time to stop running and face your life. Filling your days with activities is often an excuse to avoid problems, disappointments, or unfulfilled dreams.

My great -grandfather passed away when I was just five years old. I remember how he would ask me to sit with him on a small wooden bench as he rocked it back and forth on its uneven legs. Sometimes he spoke; sometimes he didn't. He would tell me to listen to the birds. He would pat my tiny hand. He would share his favorite saying: "An apple a day keeps the doctor away." It wasn't until I stopped racing to the imaginary finish line of career success that I realized in a quiet moment – a moment I had to force myself to take – that my great-grandfather was teaching me how to just BE.

This Week's Key To Unlock Your Potential: Amid today's culture of information overload and multi-tasking, taking time to "be" is a formidable challenge; grant yourself permission to schedule a few minutes of nothing! Pencil in a few appointments with yourself (be a trendsetter, write "alone time" in your calendar) or take as many non-working lunches as you can for one whole week. Find at least 10 or 15 minutes each day to just sit quietly sipping your drink of choice. Shun all outside input: no idle conversation, no telephone, no reading, no radio, and no television; the point is to just "be" with yourself and your own thoughts. I promise this is not as painful as it may seem; difficult, and maybe a bit frightening, but you won't know if this can help you relax into the race unless you try.

Chapter 43

Spread joy

Some people would like to make us believe that life is all work and no play. Prove them wrong. Seize every opportunity to add joy to the lives of others. A smile, a compliment, a small gift, or a card can make a world of difference in every life that is touched. Spread joy!

When I was growing up, I never stopped playing. My dad sometimes had to work the afternoon shift when I was in elementary school. I hated that I wouldn't be able to spend time with him after school, so I would sometimes sneak out of bed to watch the Three Stooges on television until he came home around midnight. We lived on the second story of a Chicago four-flat and he would hear my giggles as soon as he entered the bottom of the stairway. After we watched the show together for a while he would try to look stern as he said, "Enough is enough, I am not playing anymore; it is time for bed."

I know he enjoyed having me wait for him as much as I enjoyed our laughs together. To this day, one of my favorite ways to spread joy is to share laughter with those I love. (Even now I sometimes wait at my dad's house to greet him when he comes home from an afternoon shift.)

This Week's Key To Unlock Your Potential: Spread joy! Smile at people. See the positive side of every person and situation as you move through this week. At the end of each day write down one thing that brought you joy. And choose one thing you will do each day of this week to add joy to the day of someone else. Will you bring flowers to your mom or dad? Will you bring cookies to your best friend? Will you plan a romantic dinner with your significant other? Caution: Spreading joy may add a spring to your step, which may affect your performance in the maze of life.

Chapter 44

Exercise regularly

I cannot add enough emphasis to this area that is so vital to your well-being. If you are so busy that you won't schedule regular workouts, start by incorporating daily routines such as taking the stairs instead of the elevator, parking farther away from buildings, walking instead of driving whenever possible, even pacing and stretching at your desk while on the phone. Being busy is not an excuse to neglect your health. Exercise does not have to mean hours on an exercise bike or trips to the gym. Give yourself permission to improve your health and wellness without the guilt often associated with weight loss as the only objective. Consider the following statistics:

Y One out of four Americans does not exercise at all, reports the Centers for Disease Control and Prevention.

Υ Just ten minutes of exercise can improve your mood, according to a month-long study published by the American Psychological Association in a July 2001 article in Health Psychology magazine.

Υ The Surgeon General has reported that exercise can promote a sense of well-being, improve self-esteem, lower stress and reduce feelings of depression or anxiety.

I believe that finding the time to exercise is non-negotiable. I have tried many types of exercise, including aerobics, step aerobics, kickboxing, yoga, Pilates™ and weight training. Weight lifting helped me discover reserves of strength and stamina I never knew I had. It built my confidence and helped me center my concentration. Yoga and Pilates™ provide me with a continual challenge to improve upon what I believe to be my current best. When I take the time to take care of my body, I feel more prepared to tackle the obstacles of the day.

This Week's Key To Unlock Your Potential: Give yourself permission to improve your health and wellness without the guilt often associated with weight loss as the only objective. Do something physical each day this week. Choose something you enjoy doing, or challenge yourself to go for a walk or to take the stairs. Ask a friend to attempt a new workout class that seems interesting. This week, stay off the scale, think less of dieting and weight loss and concentrate instead on wellness.

Chapter 45

Start a "feel-good" folder

Gather positive quotes, letters of recommendation, thank-you notes and other items that make you smile and store them in a special place to review on days that you're feeling discouraged.

A friend at my first marketing job after college once told me that my independence and determination reminded her of the person she used to be before life events weighed her down. She told me that watching me bravely tackle the obstacles of the bureaucracy we worked within made her realize how she had given up on her dreams. She went home one evening and dug out all of her papers from college and letters of recommendation from colleagues and friends, and cried to see the person they once knew. This launched the fight to bring back the idealistic, intelligent, determined woman she used to be. Over the next couple of years she incorporated the former qualities she had suppressed with the wisdom she has gained and started her own successful business. This encouraged me to start my own feel-good folder, since sometimes we have to see ourselves through the lens of our past in order to remember who we are.

This Week's Key To Unlock Your Potential:
If you have been diligently completing the keys at the end of every chapter, this week will seem like a vacation. Your goal is to find a folder, box, bag or any kind of container that makes you feel good. To be creative, you may want a few sheets of colored paper to write on. Read back over the notes and lists you have been creating throughout this book. (Hint: Chapters 10, 25 and 26 are a good start) Anytime you smile or feel good about your notes, add that information to your "feel-good" folder. You can tear out the pages of your journal, transfer the information to colored paper, or make photocopies, but the point is to gather information that brings you joy. Now add cards you've received, jokes or comics, travel brochures, small mementos, or other things that make you smile and store the file in an easily accessible place. Revisit this "feel-good" folder when you are feeling lost or battered in the maze!

Chapter 46

Savor the moments

Life really is about the journey. That is a difficult concept for those of us who are always striving toward a particular goal. Savoring the moment means allowing yourself enough time to celebrate each victory before rushing on to the next event. When you're working diligently to live to your full potential, give yourself permission to accept a reward: take a day off work, have a nice dinner, visit a nearby attraction or park, plan a vacation, or throw a celebratory get-together. Above all, acknowledge that you accomplished what you struggled to attain. (More on this in Chapter 50)

When my sister and my brother-in law bought their first home, my husband and I took my sister out to lunch right after she signed the closing papers. We wanted to wish her luck but also wanted to be sure that she recognized that she should take at least an hour out of her busy day to feel proud of what she had worked so hard to achieve. Now when she looks back on the day they bought their first home, I hope she will remember how good it felt to be surrounded by people who loved and supported their achievement.

This Week's Key To Unlock Your Potential: What is your leading goal at this moment? What are you working most diligently toward attaining? Use this week to plan how you will celebrate when you have achieved this goal. Give yourself permission to accept a reward; make the celebration as important as your next goal.

Chapter 47

Choose theme songs to remember important events

Remember in high school when your classmates voted on a song that they believed captured the memories of the past four years and the hopes, wishes and dreams for the future? Or those days when you were starting a new relationship and you had "your" song? Even decades later when one of those songs begins to play, you find yourself transported to those early years. This is also a fun and simple way to remember your vacations, a new home or car purchase, a job promotion, or paying off debt. Choose a theme song for any occasion that brings you joy and every time you hear the song it will remind you of your accomplishments.

In 2001, my sister and brother-in-law planned a family vacation to South Carolina that also included my mom, dad, husband and me. We decided to drive straight through the nineteen-hour adventure in a large sport utility vehicle. As we neared Charleston by the next afternoon, everyone was hot, cranky and tired. To take our minds off the remaining time we had to spend in that truck, I turned on the radio and announced that we had to decide as a group on the theme song of the vacation. Although Destiny's Child, [I'm A] "Survivor," seemed appropriate after 18-plus hours of rough, cramped travel, we decided that wasn't the tone we were seeking. As the radio scanned the channels, Lee Ann Womack's soothing voice and verses about the ocean in "I Hope You Dance" set the perfect mood for our eight days on the shores of the Atlantic. Now even during the most stress -filled days, just hearing the song makes all of us smile thinking of our time spent together.

This Week's Key To Unlock Your Potential: Choose a theme song to remember something that is important in your life right now. It may seem silly, but learning to relax means taking yourself less seriously. If you are committed to relaxing into where you are today and plotting your course through the maze of the future, choose a song that reminds you to enjoy the journey. Every time you hear your "Rat Race Relaxer" song it will remind you to slow down and enjoy the moment.

Chapter 48

Compliment others when you admire something about them

Do you find yourself becoming jealous or envious of the qualities, lifestyles or possessions of others? Are your relationships faltering because you take out the frustrations of your own situation on those around you? Do you only associate with people whom you see as inferior in some way, just to feel better about yourself? In a society where the rewards seem to flow to the beautiful, rich, thin and young, it is sometimes difficult to avoid a feeling of competitiveness toward those you believe have more of those desirable qualities. Don't waste your energy discriminating against the praiseworthy qualities you see in someone else. Compliment others when you admire something about them and you will convert the destructive energy of jealousy into the constructive energy of self-improvement.

Start small. For example, say your next-door neighbor just went back to school to finish the degree that he began pursuing 15 years ago. Maybe you find that you're envious of your neighbor's ability to dedicate the time and finances to his own development when you are struggling to make mortgage payments. Being envious of your neighbor will only make you feel worse; it will not pay your next mortgage installment. Reverse the energy. Congratulate him for having the courage to pursue his dream and admit that you have often considered going back to school as well. This simple gesture helps you uncover your desires. By owning your dream of wanting to go back to school, it plants a seed of intention that can lead to creative ways of financing both your home and education.

This Week's Key To Unlock Your Potential:
Every day this week, make it your goal to offer a sincere compliment to someone else. Spreading false flattery is cheating; look for a quality that you truly admire in someone else and say so. Start small if necessary: say you like someone's dress, tie or hair. Build up to admiration of a quality, such as "I admire your courage." Acknowledging something you admire about another may make it easier for you to determine what you would like to improve about yourself. (You may want to revisit Chapter 15: Improve — EVERY DAY!)

Chapter 49

Remember: You are no better than anyone else is and no one is better than you are

Do you cringe at the thought of having to speak to someone you perceive as being better than you are? Do you lose your voice when you try to speak to someone with more money, more possessions, or a higher position? Do you try so hard to impress people whom you believe have more that you seem insincere or undermine your own abilities? Do you try to belittle those whom you believe have less than you? If you answer yes to any of these questions, you are forgetting that you are just as good as every other person you meet and they are just as good as you are. Every person has unique blessings and unique struggles. Your position may be different from those you encounter, but it is not necessarily better or worse.

I come from a working-class family. I was not born rich, but I was born into a stable, loving home. I was taught to strive for what would bring me joy — not necessarily money or things, but happiness. So it has always been easy for me to speak to anyone I meet, from any background, any country, any social status and any path in life. The only time I have felt nervous in the presence of another person is when I went to hear Dr. Deepak Chopra speak in Muskegon, Michigan, and had the opportunity to meet him. Deepak Chopra is a medical doctor and author of many books about the integrated health of mind, body and spirit. My nervousness was not due to his fame or accomplishments, but because I believe Dr. Chopra strives not to show others what a great person he is, but to show others how to become their best selves. When a person or situation initially seems intimidating, I concentrate on what makes me unique. Then, I am able to articulate what I have to contribute.

This Week's Key To Unlock Your Potential:
In the rat race, it is easy to lose focus of your distinctive contributions. Pay attention to how you interact with people and situations you encounter. Do you view others as better or worse than you? Are you able to articulate the qualities that make you an original? Consider how your life would change if you relinquished the need to judge and be judged by others.

Chapter 50

Look to the future, plan for the future, but live in the present

Have you ever experienced a sinking feeling of disappointment upon reaching a goal you worked so hard to achieve? When you surmount an obstacle, do you move on to other pursuits without celebrating your victory? Do you strive to save so much money for your future that you're constantly disappointed with your current standard of living? If your answer is yes, you may be living your life so far in the future that you have forgotten how to enjoy today. This is not to suggest that life should be lived haphazardly or frivolously; however, it does suggest that not one moment should be taken for granted. When we're blinded by the pursuit of goals, accomplishments and possessions, it can be difficult to see the miracles that appear along the way.

If you are sacrificing everything you have right now in the name of planning for the future, you are not living to your full potential. No one can predict the timeline of the future; it may be a day, week or many years. Set plans for the future to serve as a challenge, not an ultimatum. Ask yourself if what you are gambling for tomorrow is worth losing what you have today. Memories last only a moment; events that *could* occur are an illusion; the only way to find happiness and satisfaction today is to celebrate where you are at this moment.

This Week's Key To Unlock Your Potential: Are you gambling so much on tomorrow that you are losing what you have today? Do you enjoy life every day or are you working only so you can relax in some mirage of the future? This week, take an assessment of where you are now versus where you want to be. Weigh the sacrifices you are making with the benefits you are pursuing. Keep reaching for your dreams, but learn to systematically celebrate your place in the present. To pull ahead in the race, embrace the mystery of the future.

Chapter 51

Laugh at yourself?

Some people take themselves too seriously. Whether you are happy, sad, embarrassed, confused, or even indifferent, learn to laugh at yourself. It's impossible to know everything. It's impossible to always do the right thing. Being human means making mistakes, learning from the experience and moving on to a new lesson. To live a life of full potential, you will have to let go of the need for perfection. When all else fails, look for a reason to laugh at yourself. Let go of the need to control what will happen next. Giggle, belly laugh, laugh until you cry — but just keep laughing and the next step of your journey is destined to unfold.

Most forms of humor are amusing because they poke fun at human imperfection. That's why we laugh at things such as bloopers, blunders, marital problems, aging, and physical shortcomings. No one is perfect – accept your failings as a part of the journey and make an effort to laugh at your own imperfections.

This Week's Key To Unlock Your Potential: When was the last time you laughed so hard you almost cried? What makes you laugh? In what ways do you make others laugh? This week, find people, situations, movies, comic strips, or a comedy club and make it your goal to laugh. Also, if you tend to take yourself too seriously, think of a time that you made a seemingly big snafu but you took it in stride and it didn't ultimately hamper your success. Looking back at the situation, what, if anything, would you have done differently?

Chapter 52

Remember: You always have a choice!

The welcome pages of this book promised that it was not a book about escaping the rat race. However, it did promise to help you relax into the race, and to find some individual balance without having to opt out of the maze. The journey throughout these pages provided a map to uncover the treasures of who you are, what you have to offer, and what you want in return for running the race. Along the way, you may have also uncovered some of your internal road signs – the subtle, personal indicators that determine whether you are heading the right or wrong way. As you navigate the maze, the ability to be yourself, an original, can provide a competitive edge. Continue to unlock your potential; make a habit of reviewing the base you have built upon with each chapter and keep uncovering your individual desires.

As I continually develop my potential in the maze of life, I have often reflected upon words of wisdom passed down to me from my mother. Throughout my years, mom has willingly offered many words of advice, but there are six words that have helped me carve a unique and fulfilling life path even when it seemed out of synch with what everyone else was pursuing. As my mom always said, you might not like the options but ***Remember: You Always Have A Choice!***

This Week's Key To Unlock Your Potential: Stop. Take a few deep breaths. Review your life. Think about a situation that seems "choiceless" and begin to jot down a list of all of your options. Make a promise to yourself that as you encounter the upcoming turns in the maze of life you will consider all of your options and make reasoned, proactive choices that are the best for you. Above all, as you race toward personal success, remember, you always have a choice!

Conclusion

So you've read the Rat Race Relaxer and you're probably surprised by how quickly it seemed to end. In the Rat Race Relaxer, the end is just another beginning. Life is all about change, and change is all about the choices you make. Throughout the chapters, I have presented keys that show you how to step back and gain an overview of your situation. Now it's up to you to review what you've learned, gather your courage and start forging a path that is just right for you.

If you have taken the time to work through the goals at the end of each chapter: congratulations! By now you should have a better idea of where you've been and where your ideal path leads. The first step of your new journey is to let go of any goals that no longer support the new life choices you plan to pursue. Instead, focus your energy on how you would like to manifest your new, improved life. It's not hard to know what's right for you, but it is hard to implement the steps if you're not willing to commit to making changes. To fully implement what you've learned, you will have to refocus your attention on the things you determined to be most important in your life.

People often tell me, "But I don't know what I really want." My reply is that we usually know what we want but we think we will have to make too many sacrifices, or give up too much of what we already have to get to where we would rather be. The way to overcome the fear of having to make too many sacrifices is to commit to making changes — one step at a time. By making deliberate changes, you are able to decide every step of the way whether or not you will choose to continue. The beauty of choice is that it allows you to change your mind.

Just reading this book may have boosted your spirits, but don't be satisfied with that. Think about how much better you will feel if you incorporate some or all of these keys into your daily routine. The chapters are broken into goals that can be accomplished without adding more stress to your already full days. The longer you delay decisions, the harder it may become to discover your areas of discontent.

If you bought this book because you seem to be slipping into a deep pit of despair, my best advice would be to plan a vacation. Even if you can't afford to venture far from home, just take a couple of days off and relax while you mull over these ideas for a more enjoyable life. Vacation time helps you to recharge, replenish, rediscover your surroundings, and above all else, relax! Taking one small break from the high-speed race of life can help you find a fresh perspective.

"Vacation is absolutely out of the question," you say. Then consider reading a chapter of this book at night before you go to bed. Let your mind drift off to sleep with something new to consider. Make a promise to yourself that you will jot down ideas that occur to you in your dreams or throughout the day. If a vacation is out of the question, commute time can become your favorite time to imagine what an improved life looks like to you.

If someone else recommended this book or, even better, gave it to you as a gift, please ask that person how the Rat Race Relaxer changed his or her life. As you may remember, key 34 is to learn about the obstacles and accomplishments of others by reading, attending seminars and through personal contact. I would love to hear your stories as well. My greatest reward is hearing how I have touched the lives of others.

My closing wish is that your days, like mine, become lighter and brighter every step of the way as you confidently navigate this maze of life.

Sources

Bethards, Betty. *The Dream Book: Symbols For Self-Understanding*. Pentaluma: NewCentury Publishers, 2001.

Hansen, Cheryl J, Larry C. Stevens, and J. Richard Coast. "Exercise Duration and Mood State: How Much Is Enough to Feel Better?" *Health Psychology*. July 2001, Volume 20, Number 4.

National Center for Chronic Disease Prevention and Health Promotion. *1996 Surgeon General's Report on Physical Activity and Health*. http://www.cdc.gov/nccdphp/sgr/order.htm

Piper, Watty. *The Little Engine That Could*. New York: Grosset & Dunlap, 2001.

Rosasco, Karen, APRN, BC. 2002. Contributor to Chapter 14 of this book and Family Nurse Practitioner at Wege Institute for Mind, Body and Spirit at St. Mary's Mercy Medical Center. Grand Rapids, MI.

Suggested For Further Reading

Adrienne, Carol. *The Purpose of Your Life: Finding Your Place in the World Using Synchronicity, Intuition, and Uncommon Sense*. New York: William Morrow, Eagle Brook, 1998.

Bethards, Betty. *The Dream Book: Symbols For Self-Understanding*. Pentaluma: NewCentury Publishers, 2001.
Bower, Sharon Anthony, and Gordon H. Bower. *Asserting Yourself: A Practical Guide For Positive Change*. Cambridge: Perseus, 1991.

Bramson, Robert M. *Coping With Difficult People*. New York: Dell, 1981.

Chopra, Deepak, and David Simon. *Live Longer, Grow Younger: Ten Steps to Reverse Aging*. New York: Random House, Harmony Books, 2001.

Camp, James R. *Start With No: The Negotiating Tools That the Pros Don't Want You to Know.* New York: Random House, Crown Business, 2002.

Jeffers, Susan. *Feel The Fear And Do It Anyway.* New York: Random House, Ballantine, 1987.

McGraw, Phillip C. *Life Strategies: Doing What Works, Doing What Matters.* New York: Hyperion, 1999.

McGraw, Phillip C. *Self Matters: Creating Your Life from the Inside Out.* New York: Simon & Schuster, 2001.

Piper, Watty. *The Little Engine That Could.* New York: Grosset & Dunlap, 2001.

Ruiz, Miguel. *The Four Agreements: A Practical Guide To Personal Freedom.* San Rafael: Amber-Allen Publishing, 1997.

Sachs, Judith. *Twenty- Minute Vacations: Quick, Affordable, and Fun "Getaways" from the Stress of Everyday Life.* Chicago: Contemporary Books, Stonesong Press, 2001.

Sher, Barbara, and Barbara Smith. *I Could Do Anything If I Only Knew What It Was: How to Discover What You Really Want and How to Get It.* New York: Dell, 1994.

Weil, Andrew. *Natural Health, Natural Medicine: A Comprehensive Manual For Wellness and Self-care.* Rev. Ed. New York: Houghton Mifflin, 1995.

Williams, Redford, and Virginia Williams. *Anger Kills: Seventeen Strategies for Controlling the Hostility That Can Harm Your Health.* New York: Harper, 1993.

Index

About the Author

JoAnna Carey grew up on the South Side of Chicago, surrounded by four generations of family. Her professional background includes experience in marketing, public relations and sales, spanning the non-profit, healthcare and financial services industries (as a fully licensed stockbroker). JoAnna is an energetic, young entrepreneur who incorporates her life experience and business success to design and deliver enjoyable, influential presentations. As a speaker and author, she encourages others to face their fears, set goals, pursue their dreams and "bloom where planted."

Fun Facts about JoAnna

- Coffeehouses, bookstores, tropical beaches and trendy clothes shops are some of JoAnna's favorite places to relax.

- South Side Chicago habits die hard; listen closely and you may even catch JoAnna saying "wit" instead of "with," "cept" instead of "except," and the phrase "yous guys."

- Audiences love JoAnna's ability to tell a story, get the crowd involved and bring on fits of laughter.

- JoAnna loves to travel the world to hear about other people's stories and triumphs and share inspirational ideas for enjoying life fully. She would be honored to present at your next event.

Would you like to share a story about how the Rat Race Relaxer changed your life?

Would you like to book JoAnna as a presenter at your next event?

JoAnna Carey
Carey'D Away Enterprises, LLC
2455 Woodlake Road, Suite 4
Wyoming, MI 49509
Phone (616) 530-3787   Fax (616) 406-0944
e-mail: j.carey@att.net
Web site: www.joannacarey.com

VIP Form

To take advantage of special events, book signings, news and information, readers forums, advanced notice of upcoming products, and more...

Join the mailing list by registering at the website www.RatRaceRelaxer.com, or fill out this form and mail or fax it to:

JoAnna Carey
Carey'D Away Enterprises, LLC
2455 Woodlake Road, Suite 4
Wyoming, MI 49509
Phone (616) 530-3787   Fax (616) 406-0944

Name_____

Address_____

City_____State____Zip_____

Telephone (   )_____

E-mail address_____

How did you learn of Rat Race Relaxer?

Order Form

To order more copies of Rat Race Relaxer please fill out this form, enclose payment, and mail to:

JoAnna Carey
Carey'D Away Enterprises, LLC
2455 Woodlake Road, Suite 4
Wyoming, MI 49509

Name_____

Address_____

City_____State_____Zip_____

Telephone (   )_____

E-mail address_____

Credit Card #_____

Expiration Date_____ Signature_____

Enclosed is a: ❑Check ❑Money Order
                 ❑Mastercard ❑Visa

Description	Price	Quantity	Subtotal
Rat Race Relaxer	14.95		
Sales Tax (MI residence add $ .90 per book)	.90		
Shipping & Handling	3.95	1st book	
per additional book	1.95		
		Total	

Payment must be received with order.
Please allow 3 weeks for delivery.

Order online at www.ratracerelaxer.com or call toll free
(877) 879-8220 or fax (616) 406-0944